WORLD IN FOCUS

FOCUS ON
Ireland

ROB BOWDEN AND RONAN FOLEY

WORLD ALMANAC® LIBRARY

Please visit our Web site at: **www.garethstevens.com**
For a free color catalog describing World Almanac® Library's list of high-quality books
and multimedia programs, call 1-800-848-2928 (USA) or 1-800-387-3178 (Canada).

Library of Congress Cataloging-in-Publication Data available upon request from publisher.

ISBN 978-0-8368-6751-0 (lib. bdg.)
ISBN 978-0-8368-6758-9 (softcover)

This North American edition first published in 2008 by
World Almanac® Library
A Weekly Reader Corporation imprint
200 First Stamford Place
Stamford, CT 06912 USA

Commissioning editor: Nicola Edwards
Editor: Nicola Barber
Inside design: Chris Halls, www.mindseyedesign.co.uk
Cover design: Hodder Wayland
Series concept and project management by EASI-Educational Resourcing
(info@easi-er.co.uk)
Statistical research: Anna Bowden
Maps and graphs: Martin Darlison, Encompass Graphics

World Almanac® Library editor: Alan Wachtel
World Almanac® Library cover design: Scott M. Krall

Picture acknowledgements. The author and publisher would like to thank the following for allowing their pictures to be reproduced
in this publication: CORBIS 6, 24, 34, 36, 46, 47 (Reuters), 8 (Gianni Dagli Orti), 10 (CORBIS), 11, 41 (PictureNet Corporation), 12, 23 (Paul
McErlane/epa), 13, 31, 42 (Gideon Mendel), 14, 22, 55, 56 (Michael St. Maur Sheil), 19, 32, 39 (Richard Cummins), 35 (Alessandra Benedetti),
37 (Justin Kernoghan/epa), 38 (Geray Sweeney), 43 (Michael Short/Robert Harding World Imagery), 52 (Felix Zaska), 58 (Jason Hawkes), 59
(Howard Davies); EASI-Images *cover, title page*, 4, 5, 15, 16, 17, 18, 20, 21, 25, 26, 28, 29, 30, 33, 40, 44, 48, 49, 50, 51, 54, 57 (Chris
Fairclough/CFW Images), 27, 53 (Rob Bowden); Getty Images 45 (Chris Maddaloni/AFP); Mary Evans Picture Library 9.

The directional arrow portrayed on the map on page 7 provides only an approximation of north.
The data used to produce the graphics and data panels in this title were the latest available at the time of production.

Printed in China

1 2 3 4 5 6 7 8 9 10 09 08 07

CONTENTS

Cover: King John's Castle in Limerick stands on the banks of the River Shannon.

Title page: A landscape in County Kerry.

CHAPTER 1

Ireland – An Overview

The island of Ireland is located to the west of Great Britain. It is the second most westerly landmass in Europe, after Iceland. An ancient land steeped in folklore and legends, Ireland was under British control until the island was split into two in 1921. The northern counties remained part of the United Kingdom (UK) and are today known as Northern Ireland. The southern counties (making up about 85 percent of the landmass) formed the Irish Free State, which was renamed Eire in 1937 and then the Republic of Ireland in 1949.

TURBULENT INFANCY

Many people were unhappy with the terms of the treaty that established the Irish Free State and kept Northern Ireland as a separate state within the United Kingdom. Civil war broke out in 1922, ending in 1923 with victory for the Irish Free State. People continue to have widely different views on the split between Ireland and Northern Ireland.

The political separation of Ireland from Northern Ireland was only one element of Ireland's turbulent infancy as an independent state. Years of depopulation saw many of Ireland's most educated citizens emigrate,

▼ The Dingle Peninsula lies between Clogher Head and Sybil Head in County Kerry. Ireland's Atlantic coastline is both dramatic and rugged.

particularly to Britain and the United States, leaving the country depleted of labor. In fact, some people think that there are today at least as many Irish people living abroad as there are in Ireland. Dramatic economic changes also took place during Ireland's first decades of independence, as traditional industries declined. Rising unemployment and urban decay became a feature of many of Ireland's cities.

A COUNTRY TRANSFORMED

In 1965, Ireland signed trade agreements with Britain, and in 1973, it became a member of the European Union (EU) (called the European Economic Community, or EEC, until 1992). These events began the transformation of Ireland into a modern economy and one of the wealthiest nations in Europe. Membership in the EU brought Ireland millions of dollars worth of grants to improve its infrastructure and create new employment opportunities. Traditional industries such as mining, textiles, and food processing have been replaced with high-tech electronics, pharmaceuticals, software development industries, as well as a thriving service industry. EU membership provided new opportunities for Irish companies to trade their goods and made the country attractive to overseas companies, particularly those from the United States, with which Ireland has close connections through its history of emigration.

As Ireland's fortunes have changed, its population increased from about 3 million in 1973 to 4.1 million in 2005. This is an increase of more than 30 percent, compared with just 6.5 percent in Britain over the same period. Much of this population growth is due to Irish people returning from overseas, but recent years have seen considerable new waves of immigration from Asia and Europe in particular. The

expansion of the EU from 15 (until 2004) to 27 members by 2007 has further influenced this trend. Ireland expects to receive many immigrants from the new EU member countries over the coming years.

▲ A new retail and office complex takes shape in the center of Limerick. Ireland's booming construction industry is one of the most obvious symbols of its recent growth and success.

NEW CHALLENGES

Having survived political upheavals and the restructuring of its economy, Ireland today faces new challenges. Some of these come from its recent success. These include a rapid rise in the cost of living, particularly house prices, and severe traffic congestion as more people buy their own vehicles. Irish culture is also under pressure, with global forces diluting some traditions and making the Irish language a rarity outside the country's rural west. An increase in tourism, however, is helping to create new interest in Irish culture, enabling Irish music and Irish dance to undergo a resurgence in popularity both within and beyond Ireland. The Irish are a proud people with a strong sense of identity. As their country continues to diversify and change, this identity will undergo fresh challenges to define the Ireland of the twenty-first century.

Physical Geography

- Land area: 26,591 sq miles/ 68,890 sq km
- Water area: 537 sq miles/1,390 sq km
- Total area: 27,128 sq miles/ 70,280 sq km
- World rank (by area): 121
- Land boundaries: 224 miles/360 km
- Border countries: United Kingdom
- Coastline: 900 miles/1,448 km
- Highest point: Carrauntoohil (3,415 ft/ 1,041 m)
- Lowest point: Atlantic Ocean (0 ft/0 m)

Source: CIA World Factbook

A dancer with the Inishowen Carnival Group dances in the St. Patrick's Day Parade in Dublin. St. Patrick's Day is celebrated on March 17 every year.

ATLANTIC
OCEAN

Erris Head

ATLANTIC
OCEAN

NORTHERN
IRELAND
(to UK)

Letterkenny
DONEGAL

Killybegs Donegal
Donegal
Bay

Sligo

MONAGHAN

Dundalk

Dundalk
Bay

Irish
Sea

SLIGO

Lough
Conn

Lough
Allen

LEITRIM

CAVAN

LOUTH

Achill
Island

Castlebar

MAYO

ROSCOMMON

LONGFORD

Drogheda

Boyne

Navan

MEATH

Swords

Lough
Mask

Connaught

Lough
Ree

Mullingar

WESTMEATH

Leixlip

DUBLIN

TWELVE
BENS

Connemara

Lough
Corrib

Athlone

Celbridge

Dún Laoghaire

GALWAY

Naas

DUBLIN

Galway

REPUBLIC OF

OFFALY

Newbridge

Bray

Aran
Islands

Galway Bay

IRELAND

Shannon

KILDARE

WICKLOW
MOUNTAINS

LAOIS

Leinster

WICKLOW

Wicklow
Head

CLARE

Lough
Derg

Carlow

Arklow

Ennis

CARLOW

Loop Head

Mouth of
the Shannon

LIMERICK

Limerick

Kilkenny

TIPPERARY

KILKENNY

WEXFORD

Tralee

Munster

Clonmel

Suir

Wexford

Rosslare

KERRY

Waterford

Dingle Bay
Carrauntoohil
1,041 m
MACGILLYCUDDY'S
REEKS

Killarney

Blackwater

WATERFORD

St George's Channel

CORK

Cork

Celtic
Sea

N

0   40   80 kilometres

0   20   40 miles

Legend

★ Capital
● Cities > 100,000
● Cities > 50,000
• Cities > 25,000
· other cities
▲ Mountain

CHAPTER 2

History

Ireland's ancient history is rich and colorful. Parts of it are interwoven with elements of folklore and legend as much as known fact.

PREHISTORY AND THE VIKINGS

Archaeological finds provide evidence of a number of ancient tribes who lived in Ireland as far back as 6000–5000 B.C. One of the greatest prehistory sites is the great burial monument of Newgrange in the Boyne Valley (*Brú na Boinne*), built in around 3200 B.C. The Hill of Tara is another well-known archaeological monument. This site was traditionally the seat of Ireland's early kings.

Ireland was known to the Romans as Hibernia, but the Romans never formally attempted to conquer the country. Instead, Ireland became a Celtic country, sharing strong cultural and linguistic traits with other Celtic regions such as Wales, northern England, and Scotland. For example, Ireland's patron saint—St. Patrick— came from Wales and is credited with bringing Christianity to Ireland in around A.D. 432.

From the ninth to the eleventh centuries, Ireland was invaded by Vikings from Scandinavia. The Vikings were known for their ferocity, and they regularly raided the Irish countryside. They founded a coastal settlement in Ireland that they called *Dubh Linn*, meaning "Black Pool." In time, this area was to become Ireland's largest city and capital, Dublin. It was near Dublin, at the Battle at Clontarf in 1014, that the combined Irish forces led by the last High King of Ireland, Brian Boru, managed finally to defeat the Vikings.

ENGLISH RULE

Following the defeat of the Vikings in 1014, Ireland remained divided among a number of warring chieftains. One of these chieftains,

◀ This picture shows the view down the internal passageway of the Newgrange burial monument in the Boyne Valley.

Diarmuid McMurrough, requested help from King Henry II of England. This request resulted in the arrival in the region of Anglo-Norman soldiers in 1169 and the start of an English presence in Ireland. The role and dominance of the English in Ireland increased slowly and steadily until, by the thirteenth century, England ruled much of the country. The English had direct control over Dublin and the surrounding area but governed the rest of Ireland through a series of uneasy truces with various tribal chieftains.

The tensions in these relationships led to rebellions against English rule, the first of which occurred in Donegal and Tyrone in the early sixteenth century. The rebellion was put down, but it led the English to take a more direct approach to rule, giving large land grants to English and Scottish interests in order to extend their reach and influence. The Great Plantation of Ulster, where Scottish settlers were particularly prominent, was the largest of these regions and led to the creation of a large Protestant and Presbyterian colony in the north of Ireland. Other plantations were established in the west and south of the country, and especially in the Queen's and King's counties (now Laois and Offaly).

Over the next century, relations between the Irish and their English rulers got worse, leading to another major revolt in the mid-seventeenth century. The English sent Oliver Cromwell and his army to restore control. The English army burned a number of towns, including Drogheda, in revenge for the revolt. English rule became more forceful still and included the strong suppression of native language, culture, and religion through the Penal Laws. These laws were in place from the late-seventeenth

▲ A scene depicting the Drogheda massacre in 1649. Oliver Cromwell led the English forces as they besieged the town and killed about 3,000 people.

century until the Catholic emancipation of 1829. They effectively banned Catholicism and the speaking of the Irish language in public. Catholicism remained strong during this period, but the decline in everyday use of the Irish language—known as *Gaelige* or Gaelic—can be traced back to this time.

IRELAND 1780–1900

Under growing pressure, Britain allowed the formation of an Irish parliament throughout the eighteenth century, culminating in the short-lived Grattan's Parliament, founded in 1785. Following an uprising in 1798, the 1801 Act of Union made Ireland a part of the United Kingdom. This act of rule allowed the Irish, led by statesmen such as Daniel O'Connell (1775–1847), to have direct representation of their interests. During this period, suppression of the Irish diminished. The Catholic emancipation of 1829—during which Catholics were finally given the right to vote—is an example of their increased freedom.

Relations between Britain and the Irish were soon tested again, this time by a natural disaster. During the Great Famine of 1845–1847, Ireland's potato crop failed almost entirely as a result of a blight. Britain's reaction was late and ineffective, leading to a famine in which over one million people died of starvation and another one million people fled the country. The famine renewed the resentment of the Irish toward the British and led to new uprisings in 1848 and 1867. The latter uprising was led by a group called the Fenians, whose aim was Irish independence. The Fenian leaders were exiled to Australia but continued to influence Irish politicians within the British parliament to press for Irish home rule. Led by John Redmond and Charles Stuart Parnell, the Fenians became very active in London during the 1880s. In Ireland, a parallel movement called the Land League, led by Michael Davitt, pushed forward a program of land nationalization and reduction of power of the Anglo-Irish gentry.

FROM HOME RULE TO THE FREE STATE

By the beginning of the twentieth century, Britain's control over Ireland was weakening due to the pressure from Ireland for home rule. The exception to this was in the north of Ireland, which had a mostly Protestant population that was loyal to Britain. The majority of Ireland's people, however, were Catholic. The British recognized that home

◀ A poor Irish family searches desperately for potatoes during the Great Famine of 1845–1847.

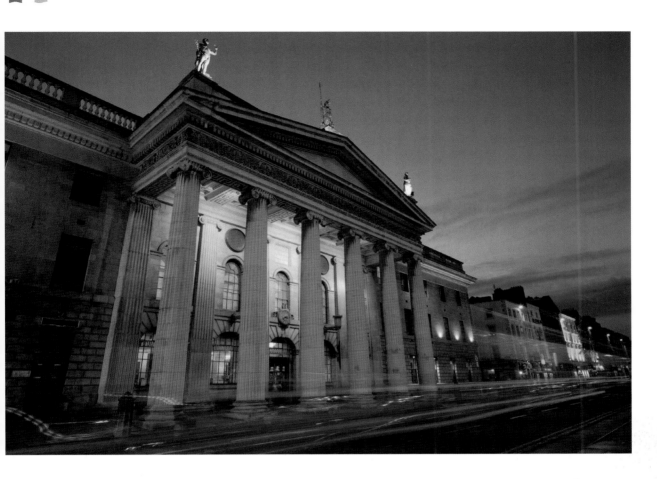

▲ The General Post Office in Dublin was the main base for the rebels during the April 1916 uprising.

rule for Ireland was inevitable. Plans to implement home rule in Ireland were mostly set by 1912, but they were delayed by the outbreak of World War I in 1914.

While Britain was distracted by World War I, the Fenians and a new organization, the Irish Republican Brotherhood (IRB), took the opportunity to begin a rebellion. These groups were committed to creating a fully independent republic that included all of Ireland. One of the leaders of the IRB, Pádraig Pearse, led the rebels as they occupied the General Post Office and other prominent Dublin buildings in April 1916. The rebels held out for a week before surrendering to the British. Pearse and most of the other leaders of the failed rebellion were executed by firing squad. Only two were spared:

Countess Markiewicz, because she was a woman; and Eamon de Valera , a future *Taoiseach,* or prime minister, and president of Ireland, because he was born in the United States.

After World War I, Irish interests became increasingly unified under the leadership of the political party Sinn Féin (We Ourselves). Sinn Féin used this support to declare the first independent *Dáil* (parliament) of Ireland. This act led to the War of Independence between Britain and Ireland in 1919–1921. A ceasefire between the two sides was reached in 1921, and negotiations began that led to the creation of the Irish Free State.

Focus on: The Irish Partition

The negotiations for Ireland's independence were to be a key point in Irish history. The main issue was the refusal of over one million Protestants in Ulster to give up British rule to a Catholic-dominated Irish state. Michael Collins and others negotiated and signed a treaty of partition with the British in December 1921. This treaty guaranteed a form of independence for the Catholic-dominated 26 southern counties as the Irish Free State. The treaty excluded the six counties of Northern Ireland, which would have a level of independent control within the British state. However, the treaty led almost immediately to the Irish Civil War (1922–1923). Michael Collins and Kevin O'Higgins led the Irish Free State against Eamon de Valera and Sinn Féin republicans who believed in a 32-county united Ireland. Michael Collins was assassinated during the course of the civil war, which was finally won by the Irish Free State.

THE TROUBLES OF THE NORTH

Southern Ireland gained full independence in 1949 and formally became the Republic of Ireland. Meanwhile, Northern Ireland remained part of the United Kingdom, a position supported by its majority Protestant population and but broadly opposed by the minority Catholic population. Up until the 1960s, life was relatively peaceful in the north, but things changed dramatically during that decade. At this time, political and economic power in Northern Ireland lay mainly in the hands of the Protestant majority. Many of the Catholic minority felt discriminated against, and, following the example of African-Americans in the United States, began to call

◀ These burned-out cars are a result of conflict in August 2006 between Protestants and Catholics in the mainly Catholic region of Bogside in Londonderry, Northern Ireland. Incidents like this are a reminder of the delicate peace that exists in Northern Ireland.

▲ This assembly line for Dell computers is in Limerick. Many high-tech companies have brought manufacturing and assembly operations to Ireland.

for equal rights. Their first civil rights marches of 1968–1969 led to resistance from members of the Protestant community, who were concerned that the movement might result in their becoming a part of a united, Catholic-dominated Ireland. Tensions between Northern Ireland's Protestant and Catholic communities escalated, with increasing violence between the two communities. In 1969, the British army was brought in to restore peace.

Peace did not come easily, however. The two sides developed paramilitary movements determined to fight for their cause through any means, including violence. The Irish Republican Army (IRA) became the main Catholic paramilitary group, while the Ulster Volunteer Force (UVF) and the Ulster Defense Force (UDF) were among those fighting the Protestant cause. The violence between the two communities, which became known as "the Troubles," was at its worst during the 1970s, when daily bombings and killings spread beyond Northern Ireland into the Republic of

Ireland and Britain. Violence continued into the 1980s and beyond, only slowing after political discussions and the 1993 Downing Street Declaration that guaranteed Protestants a vote in any potential unification. In 1994, the IRA announced a ceasefire, but the true end of violence did not take place until the fall of 2005, following more than a decade of negotiation.

RECOVERY IN THE SOUTH

In spite of the violence in Northern Ireland, the Republic of Ireland has remained politically stable. It suffered economic problems during the 1970s and 1980s but emerged in the 1990s as one of the fastest-growing and wealthiest economies in Europe. Its economic boom has slowed since 2000, but it continues to outpace many European rivals. Today, Ireland is a modern, wealthy, and increasingly cosmopolitan country.

CHAPTER 3

Landscape and Climate

Ireland covers a total area of 27,128 square miles (70,280 square kilometers), which makes it smaller than all but ten U.S. states and slightly smaller than Scotland in the United Kingdom. It shares a 224-mile (360-km) border with Northern Ireland to the north. The rest of Ireland is surrounded by the Atlantic Ocean, which includes the stretch of water between Ireland and Britain called the Irish Sea.

COASTAL HIGHLANDS

Ireland can be thought of as a saucer shape with coastal highlands forming its perimeter and a mainly flat depression toward its center. The highest point in its coastal highlands is Carrauntoohil, at 3,415 feet (1,041 meters), in the Macgillycuddy's Reeks range of County Kerry, in southwest Ireland. The Macgillycuddy's Reeks contain eight more of the ten highest peaks in Ireland. Ireland's other highlands include the Wicklow Mountains, south of Dublin, and the Twelve Bens range, in County Galway.

In the southwest of Ireland, the highlands jut into the Atlantic Ocean, forming a series of jagged peninsulas separated by rias, or former river valleys now drowned beneath the ocean. A good example of a ria is the bay of Dingle in

▼ Tourists admire the dramatic Slieve League cliffs on the Atlantic Ocean near Carrick, in County Donegal.

County Kerry. In County Donegal, located in northwestern Ireland, the highlands plunge dramatically at the sea cliffs of Slieve League. At 1,952 feet (595 m), Slieve League is one of the highest sea cliffs in Europe. The country's west coast is also characterized by a number of offshore islands, most of which are small and uninhabited. Some larger ones, such as 56-sq-mile (146-sq-km)Achill, are occupied. In sharp contrast to the country's west, Ireland's east coast is less rugged and has a number of gentle bays. Several of Ireland's most important ports, including Dublin, Drogheda, and Rosslare, are located along this eastern coastline.

WATERWAYS

Ireland's longest river, the Shannon, rises at Shannon Pot in County Cavan and flows south

▲ This picture shows the Shannon River as it flows into Limerick. The thirteenth-century King John's Castle stands in the background. West of Limerick, the Shannon flows into its estuary, which extends 70 miles (113 km) to the Atlantic Ocean.

for about 162 miles (260 km) to the Atlantic Ocean, west of Limerick. Though not very long, the Shannon River drains almost one-quarter of Ireland's land. With so much water passing through it, the river spills into marshes and bogs along much of its length and forms small lakes in several places. Ireland has over 11,000 lakes, most of which were formed by glaciers during the last Ice Age. Ireland's lakes are well known for their salmon and trout populations.

MILD CLIMATE

Ireland's position at the head of the Gulf Stream—which brings warm, moist waters from the Caribbean—means its climate is mild and wet throughout the year. Although the variation is slight, Ireland's west is slightly wetter and cloudier and more prone to

▲ These fields in County Kerry are separated by stone walls. This type of green landscape has earned Ireland its nickname—the Emerald Isle.

occasional winter storms and windier conditions, in general, than the country's east and south. The mild temperatures and regular rainfall combine with fertile soils to give Ireland some of the best grasslands in the world. The pastures of Ireland's southwest are especially prized and are the prime lands for Ireland's beef and dairy industries.

IRELAND'S LANDSCAPE

Ireland's climate determines two of its most distinctive and best-known landscape features. The first is the abundance of grass and mosses that gives the Emerald Isle its name. The second is the peat bogs that cover about one-sixth of the country and once covered much more. Ireland's peat bogs formed from the remains of decaying plants and animals that

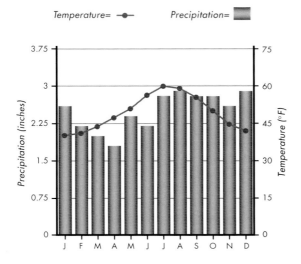

Temperature= —●—   Precipitation= ▨

▲ Average monthly climate conditions in Dublin

sank to the bottom of shallow lakes covering much of central Ireland about 10,000 years ago. Over time, this decaying material filled the lakes to a depth of about 39 feet (12 m) to create the peat bogs of today. Peat is the earliest stage of the formation of fossil fuels, and it can itself be dried and used as a source of fuel. Peat has been harvested on a small scale for hundreds of years in Ireland. Today, it is also used commercially. In 2004–2005, Ireland opened two new peat-burning power stations at Lough Ree, in County Longford, and West Offaly, in County Offaly. About half of Ireland's original peat bogs have been cleared for farming, fuel, forestry, or other uses, and only about 20 percent remain in good condition. The pressures on Ireland's peat bogs are today one of the country's greatest environmental challenges.

 Did You Know?

Many artifacts have been preserved in peat bogs, including jewelry, coins, and even an old canoe. These items give insights into Ireland's history. In addition, more than 80 human bodies have been discovered preserved in Ireland's bogs, including one dated at more than 2,000 years old. This body was found at Gallagh Bog, in County Galway, in 1821.

Focus on: Crossing Peat Bogs

Water is an essential element of a peat bog. It makes up an average of 90 percent of a peat bog by volume. This means that peat bogs are very spongy and present an obstacle to the building of infrastructure such as roads and railways. Crossing a peat bog is not a new challenge. Archaeologists have discovered the remains of ancient paths across Ireland's peat bogs that date back to 148 B.C. These paths, called *toghers*, were made of wooden planks resting across wooden rails, and they resembled a modern railway track in their design. The Corlea *togher*, located in County Longford, is one of the best examples of a *togher* in Ireland.

▶ Workers cut peat from bogs near the Wicklow Mountains, in County Wicklow, south of Dublin. Peat is harvested and burned for energy.

Population and Settlements

I reland's population in 2005 was about 4.1 million people, up from just under 3 million in 1950. Northern Ireland (part of the UK) adds a further 1.7 million, but even with this taken into account, the total population of the two regions is much smaller than it has been historically. This is due to Ireland's long history of emigration and, in particular, to the events of the Great Famine of 1845–1847. Today, however, Ireland's population is growing rapidly as returning Irish people and new immigrants arrive to take advantage of the country's recent economic prosperity.

FLUCTUATING NUMBERS

The population of Ireland (including Northern Ireland at the time) grew rapidly during the late eighteenth and early nineteenth centuries, increasing from about 4 million in 1780 to just more than 8 million by 1840. In 1845, Ireland was devastated by famine and suffered a period

 Did You Know?

Ireland has a young population, with 25 percent of its people under the age of 18. This compares with an average of 21 percent under 18 for other industrialized countries.

Population Data

- Population: 4.1 million
- Population 0–14 yrs: 21%
- Population 15–64 yrs: 68%
- Population 65+ yrs: 11%
- Population growth rate: 1.5%
- Population density: 151.1 per sq mile/ 58.3 per sq km
- Urban population: 60%
- Major cities: Dublin 1,033,000

Source: United Nations and World Bank

◀ Dublin is the most populated city in Ireland. It is the destination of many returning Irish people, as well as new immigrants. This picture shows Grafton Street, one of the city's main retail streets.

of rapid population decline, losing a quarter of its population in just a few years. Ireland struggled to recover from the famine, but during this era, people began to emigrate in large numbers, most of them going to the United States, Britain, and Australia. It is only since 1960 that Ireland—then with a population of 2.8 million—has had an increase in its population. The country's population growth has been especially fast since 1990, and it increased by 17 percent up to 2005. This is comparable with population growth in the United States over the same period (17.5 percent), but much faster than growth in the UK, which was just more than 3 percent.

Did You Know?

Since records began in 1820, more than 4.8 million Irish people have been officially admitted to the United States as permanent immigrants, half of this number before 1870. By 2005, the United States had 34 million residents claiming Irish ancestry—more than eight times the population of Ireland in the same year.

▲ Like this young boy celebrating St. Patrick's Day in San Diego, California, millions of Americans can trace their ancestry back to immigrants from Ireland.

Focus on: The Great Famine

In the nineteenth century, Ireland was almost completely dependent on the potato as its main food crop. Potatoes grew well in Ireland, but were (and still are) subject to fungal diseases known as potato blight. Outbreaks of potato blight had troubled Ireland for many years causing several periods of famine, but in 1845, a new form of blight caused widespread devastation. The blight turned the potatoes into inedible mush, and the disease spread rapidly across Ireland. Farmers were expecting a good harvest in 1845, but when they unearthed their

potatoes about one-half of the crop was inedible. The harvest of 1846 was even worse, with almost complete crop failure, and the 1847 harvest was also poor. The failed harvests were a disaster, because the country did not have enough food to support the population. Britain offered too little help, too late. The Great Famine, as it became known, caused over one million deaths due to hunger and disease and resulted in another one million people fleeing the country. The dispersal of Irish people throughout the world is directly linked to this key event in Ireland's history.

NEW DIVERSITY

Although people of Irish origin can be found across the world today, it is still comparatively unusual to find non-Irish people living in Ireland. The vast majority of the country's people are of Irish nationality. The country's last census, in 2002, found that this group made up 93 percent of Ireland's populace. People of British nationality made up the next largest group, at about 2.7 percent (103,476 people). Americans (11,384), Nigerians (8,969), Chinese (5,842), Romanians (4,978) and Spanish (4,436) were the next largest minority groups by nationality.

Sizes of minority nationalities, however, are difficult to establish accurately. In 2005, for example, estimates suggest Ireland may have had 30,000 Chinese and 50,000 Polish people living within its borders—many times the numbers on the official census records. It is clear that Ireland is becoming a more diverse society and that non-Irish immigrants account for a growing proportion of its population.

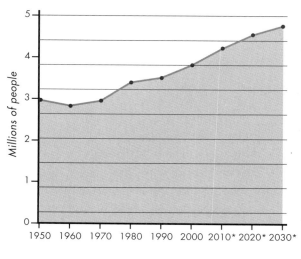

* Projected population

▲ Population growth 1950–2030

URBANIZATION

Ireland is often considered a very rural country. To some extent, this is true. In 2005, 40 percent of the country's population was rural, much higher than in the United States (19 percent) or Britain (11 percent). Nevertheless, Ireland is now predominantly urban, with 60 percent of its population living in towns and cities, and the

◀ These new arrivals in the western city of Cork are from Eastern Europe. Thousands of Eastern Europeans have emigrated to Ireland since the expansion of the EU in 2004.

▲ Workers build new housing in County Kerry. Ireland is undergoing a housing boom to try to meet the demands of its growing population.

majority of new population growth occurring in urban areas. Cork, Limerick, Waterford, and Galway are all key cities that are expanding to accommodate urban population growth. Their growth, however, is far exceeded by the capital, Dublin. The greater Dublin area includes the counties of Meath, Kildare, and Wicklow that surround the city, and it had a population of over 1.5 million in 2005. This number is expected to increase to over 2 million by 2021. This means that Greater Dublin alone accounts for about 40 percent of Ireland's population.

HOUSING

Along with Ireland's recent population growth, there has been a boom in housing development in the country. Many cities are expanding outward onto surrounding farmland or merging with other settlements. Inner city areas, such as Dublin's former industrial docks, are also being redeveloped to provide new housing—much of it luxury city apartments. In spite of extensive building programs, the country still has a housing shortage. This shortage has driven prices up dramatically in recent years. A 2006 poll by the national broadcaster RTÉ found that 90 percent of the country's people felt house prices were too high in Ireland. Today, even modest housing is unaffordable for lower-income earners in the cities, forcing people to move into neighboring areas and travel into the cities to work. This adds to problems of traffic congestion and is driving up property prices in rural areas. Public opinion is now growing in the country for the government to intervene in the housing market.

CHAPTER 5

Government and Politics

The continued separation of Ireland from the six counties that make up Northern Ireland means that politics is never far from people's thoughts in Ireland. The country's own political system itself is also frequently under scrutiny, and scandal and corruption never seem to be far from Ireland's headlines.

POLITICAL STRUCTURE

Ireland has a two-chamber system of government similar to that of Britain. The main chamber is the *Dáil Éireann,* or parliament, which consists of 166 members elected by popular vote for a five-year term. The smaller Senate, or *Seanad Éireann,* has 60 members. Eleven of its members are nominated by the prime minister, 6 are elected by university graduates, and 43 are elected in Senate panel elections; Senate members also serve a five-year term. Ireland's head of state is the president, who appoints both the prime minister (*Taoiseach*) and the cabinet. Mary McAleese succeeded Mary Robinson as president in 1997 and won a second seven-year term in 2004. The country's prime minister is Bertie Ahern.

POLITICAL PARTIES

The largest party in Ireland is Fianna Fáil, which dominated Ireland's politics through the last century and currently holds 81 of the 166 seats in the *Dáil Éireann*. Because this is not quite enough to form a government, Fianna Fáil currently governs in coalition with the 8 seats held by the Progressive Democrats. The main opposition parties in Ireland are Fine Gael (31 seats) and Labor (21 seats). In recent years, support has grown for the Green Party (6 seats)

◀ Leinster House—located on Kildare Street, in Dublin—was built in 1745. Since 1924, it has been the seat of the Irish parliament. It also serves as the Senate building when parliament is out of session.

and Sinn Féin (5 seats). Sinn Féin is a controversial party to some people, because it is associated with Northern Ireland and, more specifically, with the IRA, a terrorist group committed to ending British rule in Northern Ireland and uniting all of the island under one government. Sinn Féin shares these goals, but its leaders insist it is a respectable political party that does not believe in any form of violence. Sinn Féin leaders point to their vital role in persuading the IRA to give up its armed struggle, a goal that was finally achieved on July 28, 2005. Today, Sinn Féin is the only party represented across the whole of the island of Ireland (including Northern Ireland). It is also the fastest-growing party in Ireland.

Focus on: The Peace Process

Ireland's prime minister, Bertie Ahern, has been a key figure in the struggle to bring peace to Northern Ireland. Together with British prime minister Tony Blair, Ahern was instrumental in working with the different political sides in Northern Ireland to reach the landmark Good Friday Agreement (also known as the Belfast Agreement) on April 10, 1998. This agreement set out a path for Northern Ireland to form its own government—the Northern Ireland Assembly—and for greater cooperation with both Ireland and Great Britain. In 2002, disagreements led to the collapse of the Northern Ireland Assembly, but in April 2006, Bertie Ahern and Tony Blair again combined forces to set out a timetable for self-governance and lasting peace.

► Bertie Ahern (left), the prime minister of Ireland, and Tony Blair, the British prime minister, have been key figures in the efforts to bring political stability to Northern Ireland.

PROPORTIONAL REPRESENTATION

Ireland's politicians are elected using a voting system called proportional representation (PR). Under PR every person over 18 has a single vote to elect representatives in a constituency (a political or electoral district). Between three and five representatives are elected for each constituency. Voters rank their choices, including as many candidates as they like. When the votes are counted, once a candidate has a sufficient number of votes, he or she is elected as a representative. The votes are then recounted to take account of voters' second choices. This process continues through third choices and beyond until all the representatives for a constituency have been decided. This model of PR may seem complicated, but is favored by Ireland, because it is thought that under it most voters get at least one of their preferred representatives elected.

CORRUPTION AND MISTRUST

Political scandals and charges of corruption of government ministers and politicians have long plagued Ireland's politics. Many of the country's scandals have been linked to property deals in which politicians have been paid money by developers, apparently in return for planning favors. One of the best-known examples of alleged government corruption involved former prime minister Charles Haughey, who died in June 2006. Two public inquiries have revealed that while in office between 1987 and 1993,

▼ Sinn Féin's Sean Crowe (center) hugs his wife after being elected to the Dublin South West seat in the May 2002 Republic of Ireland general elections.

▲ The National Development Plan (NDP) is one of many projects in Ireland partly funded by the EU. This sign indicates an NDP road improvement program.

Haughey received about U.S.$14.4 million from wealthy businessmen.

IRELAND AND THE EU

Ireland's membership in the EEC—later the EU—has been a major influence on domestic politics and, indeed, all aspects of Irish life. At the time Ireland joined, the average Irish person was one of the poorest in Europe, with a weekly income of just U.S.$50—less than two-thirds of the EU average. As a result, Ireland qualified immediately for massive EU investment. Between 1973 and 2003, Ireland received a large amount of money to invest in economic and social projects ranging from road building and new rail lines to community theater and unemployment retraining programs.

By 2003, Ireland had received about U.S.$35.7 billion more from the EU than it had paid in contributions, and the country's average weekly income had reached U.S.$540, among the highest in Europe. In 2004, ten new member states joined the EU, many of them hoping to benefit like Ireland. But because of greater competition for EU funds, Ireland may find itself losing out to newer members. This will place greater pressure on the country's politicians who, until recently, have been able to rely on generous EU funding to deal with challenging issues such as unemployment.

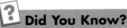 **Did You Know?**

On January 1, 2002, Ireland adopted a new European currency, the euro ( ), together with 11 other European countries. The Irish pound (punt) disappeared almost overnight.

CHAPTER 6

Energy and Resources

Ireland has very limited reserves of conventional fuels, such as gas and coal, to meet its energy needs. As a result, 87 percent of its total energy requirements are met by imported fuels. The country's nonenergy resources are also limited, with farmland and fisheries being by far its most significant assets.

ENERGY HUNGRY

Ireland's economic growth since 1990 has led to a massive increase in energy demands. This demand is partly driven by new manufacturers and businesses establishing themselves in Ireland, but is also due to a rising standard of living and increased consumption by the population. Between 1990 and 2004, energy demand in Ireland increased by 59 percent. (During 1990–2002, energy demand increased by 19 percent in the United States and by 7 percent in Britain). The forecasts for future

▼ This equipment is used for extracting methane gas from a landfill site in County Clare. The use of gas generated by waste is one of the forms of energy efficiency being promoted by Ireland's government.

energy demand expect growth between 2005 and 2020 to slow to about 38 percent, but this is still a large increase.

ENERGY SOURCES

Historically, Ireland has relied on coal and peat to meet its energy needs. In 1990, coal provided 23 percent of Ireland's energy, while peat provided 14.4 percent. Since then, these figures have dropped considerably, to 12.9 percent for coal and 3.8 percent for peat in 2004. The decline in their share of Ireland's total energy is due to the closure of older coal- and peat-fired power stations and to the strong growth of oil and natural gas as alternatives. From 1990 to 2004, Ireland's consumption of oil increased by 95 percent, and its share of total energy use increased from 44.5 percent to 55.8 percent. Consumption of natural gas grew even faster—by 153 percent—mostly due to its use for generating electricity. The share of Ireland's total energy produced from natural gas rose from 15.4 percent in 1990 to 24.3 percent by 2004.

Future energy forecasts up to 2020 predict that Ireland's use of coal and peat will continue to decline, while its oil and particularly natural gas consumption will continue to rise. Ireland has proven reserves of about 699 billion cubic feet (19.8 billion cubic meters) of natural gas, and several offshore gas fields are currently being prepared for commercial extraction. Ireland's fastest growing energy sector from 2005 to 2020, however, is expected to be renewable energies such as wind power, wave power, and hydroelectric power (HEP). If, as predicted, power produced from these sources increases by 146 percent by 2020, then their share of Ireland's total energy will increase to 3.3 percent, compared to 2.2 percent in 2004.

▲ A motorist inserts money into a solar-powered parking meter in Clonmel. Ireland's government is seeking ways to increase its share of energy from renewable sources such as solar power.

 Did You Know?

As an economy, Ireland is relatively good at using energy efficiently. The level of income generated per unit of energy in Ireland is about 1.4 times greater than in Britain and 2.5 times greater than in the United States.

ELECTRICITY PRODUCTION

Natural gas, coal, and oil account for almost all electricity generation in Ireland, but Ireland also imports electricity. Ireland's electricity importing is expected to increase in the future. Renewable energies account for an ever-growing proportion of the country's electricity generation, and by 2020, they are expected to account for 8.3 percent of electricity, with most of this increase coming from wind power.

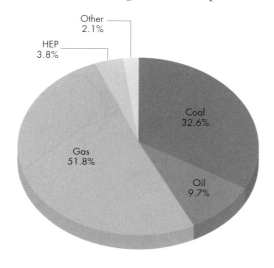

Other
2.1%

HEP
3.8%

Coal
32.6%

Gas
51.8%

Oil
9.7%

▲ Electricity production by type

Focus on: Renewable Energy

Ireland's earliest renewable energy came in the form of hydroelectric power (HEP). The first HEP installation at Ardnacrusha, in County Clare, was opened in October 1929. The country now has several HEP installations, and they produced 3.8 percent of its electricity in 2002. Wind energy in Ireland grew from virtually nothing in 1992 to a capacity of almost 500 megawatts by the end of 2005. (HEP by contrast produced 241 MW.) Much of the increased wind-power capacity in 2004 came from the opening of Ireland's largest wind farm at Meentycat, in County Donegal, and its first offshore wind farm located 6 miles (10 km) off the coast at Arklow, in County Wicklow. Strong growth continued in 2005. Ireland has one of the highest wind-power potentials in the world.

▼ A stone quarry north of Limerick provides stone for use in Ireland's construction and road-building industries.

Energy Data

- Energy consumption as % of world total: 0.1%
- Energy consumption by sector (% of total):
  Industry: 23.8%
  Transportation: 35.5%
  Agriculture: 2.4%
  Services: 13.5%
  Residential: 23%
  Other: 1.8%
- CO_2 emissions as % of world total: 0.2%
- CO_2 emissions per capita in tons per year: 12.3

Source: World Resources Institute

MINERAL RESOURCES

Ireland has commercially viable deposits of several minerals, the most significant of which are zinc, lead, and gypsum. In 2005, Ireland produced about 41 percent of Europe's zinc concentrate and 27 percent of its lead concentrate. The country's gypsum industry received a boost in 2005 when an underground mine opened in County Monaghan. Copper, gold, silver, barites, dolomite, and talc are other minerals that are (or have been) mined in small quantities in Ireland.

LAND AND SEA

Ireland's farmland and fisheries have long been an important resource. Ireland's farm products are respected worldwide. Its fisheries are also important, although less so than in the past, as a result of EU quotas on fish catches to conserve stocks. In 2005, the Irish fishing fleet was limited by the rules of the EU Common Fisheries Policy to 55 days at sea per year. The Irish fishing industry continues to modernize and develop. The recent work on Killybegs Port, in County Donegal, will make it the largest seafood port in Europe. Aquaculture—the farming of fish and shellfish—has experienced strong growth in Ireland since its introduction in the 1970s, with output increasing from 29,200 tons (26,500 metric tons) in 1990 to a peak of 67,200 tons (61,000 metric tons) in 2002.

▲ This commercial fish farm lies off the coast of County Kerry. Fish farming makes up an increasing proportion of Ireland's total fish production.

 Did You Know?

The seven offshore turbines installed at Arklow Bank Offshore Wind Park in 2004 were the largest in the world at the time. Each turbine stands about 407 feet (124 m) high and has a rotor diameter of 341 feet (104 m). A jumbo jet, in comparison, has a wingspan of about 210 feet (64 m). These turbines produce enough electricity to power 16,000 average Irish homes.

CHAPTER 7

Economy and Income

Ireland's economy has undergone a revolution since the 1980s, transforming itself from one of the weakest to one of the strongest in Europe. Between 1990 and 2004, for example, Ireland's economy (measured by its GDP) almost quadrupled in value, with average annual growth of 6.7 percent and a high of 10.25 percent growth between 1997 and 2000. In comparison, average annual economic growth from 1990 to 2004 for Britain was 2.3 percent, and for the United States 3.1 percent.

TRADITIONAL ECONOMY

As recently as 1980, agriculture and industry accounted for 51 percent of employment in Ireland and 48 percent of the country's domestic economy. Agriculture is Ireland's traditional industry, and the country is well known for its high-quality beef and dairy produce. Ireland's industry was focused primarily on the harvesting and processing of natural resources such as peat and timber, as well as the mining of minerals including zinc, lead, gypsum, and copper. Manufacturing industries in Ireland were traditionally small-scale and included textiles, food, and beverages.

ECONOMIC TRANSFORMATION

In 1965, Ireland signed the Anglo-Irish Free Trade Agreement with Britain, and in 1973, it became a member state of the EEC. These two key events removed trade barriers, such as taxes and quotas on trade, and helped transform Ireland's economy, creating new export opportunities for Irish goods. A government body called the Industrial Development Authority (IDA) worked to encourage the growth of industry in Ireland and to persuade foreign companies to locate their operations in Ireland. Engineering, electronics, and pharmaceutical industries were among those attracted to set up in Ireland, leading to substantial growth in manufacturing and industry in the country at a time when most other European nations were suffering a decline. As a result, manufacturing and industry's share of Ireland's economy grew from 35 percent in 1973 to 41 percent in 2003. This may not seem like a big jump, but in Britain and the United States, the economic contribution of manufacturing and industry declined over the same period. In Britain, it dropped from 42 to 26 percent, while, in the United States, it fell from 34 to 22 percent.

◀ Dorrus Farmhouse cheese is coated in salt water before being packaged and stored. This small cheese factory in Dorrus, in County Cork, is one of many specialized dairy producers in Ireland.

Agriculture has been unable to sustain its contribution to Ireland's economy, falling from 18 percent of GDP in 1973 to just 3 percent by 2003. It remains an important sector, however, employing about 6 percent of the country's workforce in 2003 and increasingly specializing in high-value, quality produce and meeting the growing demand for organic goods.

FOREIGN INVESTMENT

Ireland's geographical location between the major markets of Europe and North America, its educated workforce, and its relatively low taxes have attracted many overseas companies to invest in the country since the early 1990s. High-tech sectors in the country, such as the computer, software, and biomedical industries, have undergone particular growth. In Leixlip, to the west of Dublin, for example, the U.S. computer chip giant Intel has invested in huge facilities, the biggest outside the United States.

Other well-known high-tech companies with substantial operations in Ireland include Microsoft, Apple, and Dell.

▲ These lab technicians wear special suits to protect the sensitive semiconductors being manufactured at this Intel computer-chip factory in Leixlip.

❓ Did You Know?

Ireland's recent economic success has been compared to that of several Southeast Asian economies including South Korea, Taiwan, and Singapore. These economies were called the "East Asian Tiger economies," and Ireland has since become known as the "Celtic Tiger."

Economic Data

- 🗁 Gross National Income (GNI) in U.S.$: 137,761,000,000
- 🗁 World rank by GNI: 35
- 🗁 GNI per capita in U.S.$: 34,280
- 🗁 World rank by GNI per capita: 12
- 🗁 Economic growth: 5%

Source: World Bank

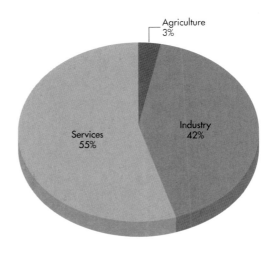

Agriculture 3%
Industry 42%
Services 55%

▲ Contribution by sector to national income

Service industries, including telemarketing and teleservices, insurance, and banking companies, have also invested heavily in Ireland. In Dublin, the Irish Financial Services Center (IFSC) has been particularly successful.

Although sectors such as information technology (IT) and financial services are hugely beneficial to Ireland's economy, some analysts believe that the country depends too much on foreign investment in these areas. One reason this may be a problem is that companies could relocate if more competitive locations (such as China) emerged. Ireland works to adapt to these pressures by improving the efficiency and quality of the services and infrastructure needed by these companies.

? Did You Know?

More than one-half of the world's top 50 banking corporations and one-half of its top 20 insurance companies have offices in Dublin's IFSC. This makes the IFSC one of the world's premier financial centers.

Focus on: The IFSC

The Irish Financial Services Center (IFSC) was established in 1987 by Ireland's government with the approval of the EU. Its aim was to boost the country's economy by creating a zone in Dublin that would attract new service industries such as banks, insurance companies, and trading companies. The area's infrastructure was redeveloped, and companies choosing to invest in the IFSC were offered a lower rate of corporate tax (10 percent, as opposed to the normal 12.5 percent) up until 2006. The IFSC has been a great success, and some analysts estimate that over a trillion euros are now traded through the IFSC annually. Although taxes for IFSC companies have reverted to 12.5 percent, this is still lower than taxes in other European nations, such as Germany (38.9 percent), France (34.33 percent), and Britain (30 percent). This means the IFSC remains attractive to overseas investors looking for a European base. It continues to expand.

▶ These modern office buildings are part of the IFSC. The IFSC is located in a part of Dublin that used to be a dock area.

RISING INCOMES, RISING COSTS

The average annual income of a person in Ireland nearly tripled between 1990 and 2004. By 2004, the average income of about U.S.$34,280 was almost 25 percent higher than the average for the Eurozone countries (the 12 countries, including Ireland, that share the euro currency). In 1990, Ireland's annual income per person was 32 percent below average. With rising incomes have come rising costs, particularly in the housing market. The cost of an average house in Ireland increased from U.S.$87,500 in 1996 to U.S.$370,000 in 2005.

EMPLOYMENT

Ireland presently has low unemployment and suffers from a shortage of labor needed to maintain its current strong growth. In recent years, this labor shortage has been filled by non-Irish immigrants. By October 2005, Ireland had almost 160,000 noncitizens in its workforce. These people made up about 8 percent of the country's workforce. Most noncitizens working in Ireland find employment in relatively low-paid jobs in the catering, hospitality, manufacturing, health-care, education, and agricultural sectors. They play a vital role in the country's economy, and forecasts suggest their numbers will continue to rise,

especially following the expansion of the EU to 25 members in 2004. The majority of noncitizens entering Ireland in 2004–2005 to find work came from new EU member states. Their number more than tripled in less than a year.

? Did You Know?

The high cost of housing in Ireland has fueled building in the country. More than one-third of all houses in the country were built between 1996 and 2005.

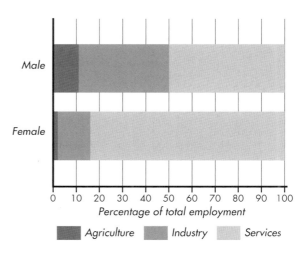

Percentage of total employment

■ Agriculture   ■ Industry   ■ Services

▲ Labor force by sector and gender

► Expensive luxury cars are one sign of Ireland's recent prosperity, but not everyone in the country is sharing in the wealth.

CHAPTER 8

Global Connections

Ireland has always maintained a neutral stance in international relations. For example, it played no part in World War II. Ireland does, however, play an important international role within groups such as the United Nations (UN) and the EU. Ireland's role in UN peacekeeping missions is a good example of its commitment to international affairs. Irish troops have taken part in peacekeeping missions ranging from early deployments in 1960s Congo to more recent actions in Lebanon, Sierra Leone, and Namibia.

IRELAND'S INTERNATIONAL ROLE

Irish nongovernmental organizations (NGOs) also feature heavily in emergency relief, aid, and long-term development work around the world. In the early days of the Irish state, most Irish NGOs were missionary organizations involved in charitable and educational work in Africa, Asia, and South America. More recently, Irish NGOs and agencies such as Concern, Trócaire, Gorta, and Goal have all become major forces in overseas aid and international development. Individuals from Ireland have also played significant international roles, including a former president of Ireland, Mary Robinson, who became UN High Commissioner for Human Rights (1997–2002). Other well-known Irish activists include Bono, the lead singer from the Irish rock band U2, and Bob Geldof, both of whom have been vocal in campaigns to alleviate poverty in Africa and other developing regions.

IRISH EMIGRATION

The Great Famine sparked mass emigration from Ireland to many parts of the English-speaking world. While many people may trace their Irish ancestry back to this event, it was not the first example of Irish emigration. Beginning in the late eighteenth century, potato-pickers routinely left northern counties such as Donegal,

◀ These Irish soldiers are on duty for the UN in Yaroun, in southern Lebanon, as part of a peacekeeping force deployed to provide security following Israel's withdrawal from Lebanon in 2000.

Focus on: Bob Geldof

Bob Geldof began his public life as the lead singer of Irish pop band the Boomtown Rats but became internationally famous as one of the key organizers of the Live Aid benefit concerts in 1985. Live Aid was motivated by horrific images of suffering during a famine in Ethiopia, and it resulted in a best-selling record and huge open-air concerts to raise funds for the famine victims. Over U.S.$50 million was given worldwide, saving millions of lives. Since Live Aid, Bob Geldof has remained involved in campaigns to improve the well-being of people living in Africa. In 2004, he became part of a campaign to reduce debt for the world's poorest countries. His involvement included meetings with world leaders such as George W. Bush and Tony Blair. In 2005, 20 years after the original Live Aid concerts, Geldof organized Live 8, a series of simultaneous concerts in nine cities around the world to raise awareness of global poverty and money to fight it.

▲ Bob Geldof is one of the best-known Irish people in the world, because he has worked for more than 20 years to fight poverty in Africa.

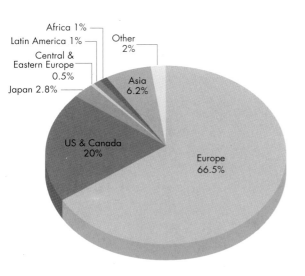

▲ Destination of exports by major trading region

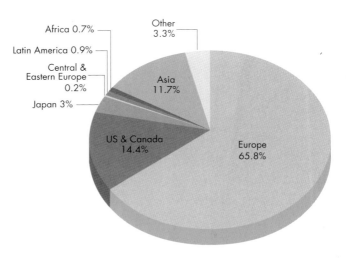

▲ Origin of imports by major trading region

Derry, and Antrim to work in Scotland, and emigration to England began in the early nineteenth century to meet the new labor demands of the Industrial Revolution. Liverpool, Manchester, and Birmingham attracted particularly large Irish populations at this time.

Wherever the Irish have emigrated, they have created their own communities, blending elements of their own culture with that of their new homeland. This is especially true in North America, where a strong Irish-American culture has developed. Many famous and influential people in the United States have Irish ancestry, including the presidents John F. Kennedy, Ronald Reagan, and Bill Clinton; movie stars; and rappers.

▼ Former U.S. president Bill Clinton plays a round of golf at Ballybunion Golf Club, in County Kerry, in May 2001. Clinton is one of many famous Americans who trace their ancestry to Ireland.

Beyond North America and Britain, Irish people are found across the world in smaller numbers. One of the first Irish people to make it to South America was a military man, Colonel Bernard O'Higgins. O'Higgins is important in South American history because his alliance with Simón Bolívar led to the independence of countries such as Bolivia, Venezuela, Peru, and Chile. Irish people have also been prominent in Commonwealth countries such as Australia and New Zealand. Many of the first Irish people to live in Australia were convicts who were sent to the Australian penal colony for petty crimes or for their political beliefs; the last ship ever to bring convicts to Australia in 1867 was full of rebel Fenians.

EXPORTING THE IRISH

Elements of Irish culture such as the welcoming Irish bar, or public house, have been exported across the world from the Czech Republic to Cambodia. Another famous Irish export is Guinness, a beer now brewed around the world. Culturally, Irish music is popular

worldwide. Ireland's big stars include U2 and the Corrs. The Irish have also excelled in international competition in sports such as horse racing, motor racing, golf, and soccer. Players of Gaelic sports, such as Gaelic football and hurling, have their own clubs in Brussels, in Belgium; Toronto, in Canada; and even Taipei, in Taiwan.

NEW CONNECTIONS

Increased prosperity in Ireland together with greatly enhanced global transportation and communications are allowing the Irish to form many new connections in the twenty-first century. For example, Irish investors have become heavily involved in overseas property markets in Britain, Spain, Portugal, Eastern Europe, and South Africa. The return of former emigrants to take advantage of Ireland's recent economic growth is creating new international connections. This is further enhanced by the recent influx of immigrants to Ireland in the 1990s, many of them asylum seekers from various areas of conflict, including Bosnians, Somalis, and Kurds. More recently, newly arrived communities in Ireland included large numbers of people from China, Poland, Lithuania, and Russia.

On the streets of Dublin, Cork, and even Ireland's smaller cities, there are now international restaurants and stores that offer a taste of the wider world. It is not unusual to see a traditional Irish pub next to a Japanese sushi restaurant and a Russian food store. But the speed with which new communities have emerged in Ireland has also raised some tensions with local people. Integrating newly arrived people into the new multicultural Ireland represents a considerable challenge.

▼ More than one half of the competitors in the World Irish Dancing Championships come from outside Ireland.

? **Did You Know?**

John Ford—father of Henry Ford, who founded the Ford Motor Company—emigrated to the United States after being evicted from Ballinascarty, in County Cork, in 1847.

CHAPTER 9

Transportation and Communications

Residents and visitors frequently complain about Ireland's transportation system, which they consider outdated and overused. Dublin has some of the worst traffic in western Europe. Since 2000, Ireland has embarked on numerous initiatives to modernize its transportation and communications systems to meet the needs of its growing economy.

CANALS AND RAILWAYS

The Newry Canal (built in 1745) linked the coalfields near Lough Neagh to the Irish Sea. It was the first canal in the British Isles. The last commercial use of Ireland's canals was in the 1950s, as the railways took over. Ireland's first railway, which connected Dublin to the seaport at Kingstown (now Dún Laoghaire), was built in 1838. The country's rail network reached its peak in about 1920 but has declined ever since due to competition from roads. In the 1950s and 1960s, major parts of Ireland's rail network closed. Today's public rail network provides only key services connecting Dublin and other cities, such as Cork, Waterford, Limerick, and Sligo. A rail line between Dublin and Belfast in Northern Ireland, is jointly operated by Irish Rail and Northern Ireland Railways.

Transport & Communications Data

- Total roads: 59,489 miles/95,736 km
- Total paved roads: 59,489 miles/95,736 km
- Total unpaved roads: 0 miles/0 km
- Total railways: 2,058 miles/3,312 km
- Airports: 36
- Cars per 1,000 people: 382
- Cellular phones per 1,000 people: 880
- Personal computers per 1,000 people: 421
- Internet users per 1,000 people: 317

Source: World Bank and CIA World Factbook

◀ The new Boyne Bridge near Drogheda is part of the M1 highway. This is one of many infrastructure projects to improve transportation in Ireland.

? Did You Know?

Ireland's earliest rail line between Dublin and Kingstown (now Dún Laoghaire) was one of the world's first commercial passenger lines when it opened in 1838. It is still in use today.

ROAD TRANSPORTATION

Motor vehicles dominate transportation in Ireland today. With the country's recent prosperity, its number of vehicles has risen from 270 per 1,000 people in 1990 to almost 400 per 1,000. This increase has brought significant problems because of Ireland's relatively small size and poor road network. The country has few highways and with much of the population concentrated in urban areas, traffic in the areas can be especially bad.

The National Development Plan (NDP) is a major government initiative that includes improvements to Ireland's road infrastructure. A primary aim of the NDP is to ensure that all main cities are connected by multiple-lane roads by 2015. The M1 highway linking Dublin to Belfast in Northern Ireland is one of the major NDP projects. By 2006, about two-thirds of this project was completed. When finished in 2010, the M1 is expected to reduce travel time between Dublin and Belfast to less than two hours.

SUSTAINABLE TRANSPORTATION

Several forms of transportation have been introduced in Greater Dublin in order to reduce car use in and around the capital. The first of these was the DART (Dublin Area Rapid Transit) system, an urban rail line opened in the 1970s that links the northern and southern coastal suburbs. More recently, two light rail routes known as the Luas (meaning speed) were opened in 2004. The Luas has been heavily used since its opening, carrying an estimated 60,000 passengers daily. In 2005, Ireland launched a plan called Transport 21 for the period from 2005 to 2015, in which the Luas plays a role. The plans include linking the existing lines and extending services with new lines. To reduce the need for cash transactions, a payment card was introduced to Luas in 2005. It is the first step toward an integrated payment system for Ireland's public transportation.

▲ A passenger boards one of the new Luas light-rail trams that began to serve Dublin in 2004.

? Did You Know?

Dublin's old tram lines closed in 1959. In 2004, modern Luas light-rail trams began to run in Dublin once again in order to promote more sustainable transportation.

AIR TRAVEL

Ireland's two key international airports are in Dublin, in the east, and Shannon, in the west. Dublin Airport is particularly busy. In 2006, plans were approved for a new runway to cope with increasing demand. Shannon's main international traffic is transatlantic, with connections to the United States. Ireland's other international airports, which deal mainly with short-haul European traffic, are in Cork and Knock. The country has domestic airports in Sligo, Kerry (Farranfore), Waterford, and Galway.

Ireland's national carrier, Aer Lingus, has been in business since the 1930s and flies to a number of European and U.S. destinations. More recently, however, Ryanair has become the better known Irish-owned airline for its major role in revolutionizing air travel in Europe.

Did You Know?

In 2005–2006, Ryanair carried about 25 million passengers a year. By 2012, this number is expected to reach almost 70 million a year.

Formed in 1985, Ryanair specializes in low-cost flights to smaller airports across Europe, a successful formula that has made it one of the world's largest and most profitable air carriers.

COMMUNICATIONS TECHNOLOGY

Technology and communications have played key roles in Ireland's economic success. In spite of this, public use of the Internet (measured by users per 1,000 people) in 2004–2005 was less than half that of the United States, Britain, Denmark, and Sweden and lower than in France and Germany. Internet use in Ireland is likely to increase with the spreading of high-speed broadband technology across the country.

Four main companies dominate Ireland's cellular phone market, which in 2006 had about 4 million subscribers. Cellular phones are particularly popular among Ireland's younger generations for both calling and text messaging. In 2006, Irish users sent about 3.6 billion text messages.

◄ Passengers disembark from a Ryanair jet. Ryanair has become one of the most influential airlines in Europe as a result of its inexpensive fares.

NATIONAL MEDIA

Ireland's national broadcasting corporation, RTÉ (*Radio Telefís Éireann*), provides two TV channels (RTÉ One and Two). The country's independent channels include TV3 and the Irish language channel TG4. RTÉ broadcasts four national radio stations, including an Irish language service, and the country also has a number of local independent stations. Ireland's print media is dominated by the *Irish Times* and the *Irish Independent*. Many British newspapers now produce an Irish version.

DIGITAL SERVICES

Digital television is rapidly increasing its share of the market in Ireland, bringing hundreds of new channel options. British-based channels are particularly popular. By 2006, about 28 percent of the 1,350,000 Irish households with a television had switched to digital television services provided by cable or satellite.

▲ This touch-screen payphone on a Dublin street also provides Internet access and e-mail capability.

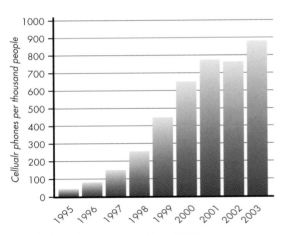

▲ Cellular phone use, 1995–2003

Focus on: Ennis E-town

In the late 1990s, the small town of Ennis, in County Clare, won a national competition to be developed as Ireland's first experimental e-town—a town designed to maximize the use of information technology in daily life. Between 1997 and 2002, a total of U.S.$22.2 million was invested to develop a town network that was completely connected to the Internet by home computers and able to exchange information and services electronically. A total of 20,000 residents, 610 businesses, and 13 schools, together with 87 community organizations and 2 local authorities, took part in the experiment and continue to develop their IT use in the town today.

CHAPTER 10

Education and Health

Ireland's education and health systems are similar to those of Britain and other European countries and provide good standards of service. Both are undergoing changes and modernization to meet the changing demands of the population and the times.

PRIMARY EDUCATION

Primary schooling in Ireland is provided free by the government, with most children starting at the age of four or five and attending for about seven years up to the age of 12. An increasing number of children in the country attend preschools or playgroups before entering school, but these are privately run and expensive for lower-income families. Some primary schools are *Gaelscoil*, or Irish language schools. These have been growing in popularity with the renewal of interest in the Irish language. Ireland's primary schools were traditionally run by various religious orders, but this is less common today. A new, government-funded but specifically nondenominational primary system called Educate Together has emerged in recent years. One problem facing all primary schools is the demand for places, especially in Ireland's growing suburban communities that are popular with young families.

SECONDARY EDUCATION

Secondary schooling in Ireland begins at about 12 or 13 years of age and typically lasts for six years. Secondary school is marked by two main exams. Students take the Junior Certificate after three years of secondary schooling, and they take the Leaving Certificate after three more years. Many students take a transition year after the Junior Certificate to do noncurricular subjects such as archaeology, philosophy, law, and civic and social education, as well as to obtain some work experience. Most secondary schooling in Ireland is state-funded, but there

◀ Young children pray during a lesson at St. Brigid's Girls' School, in Dublin.

► Trinity College is the oldest and most prestigious university in Ireland. This picture shows Trinity's main library.

are a also vocational and technical schools and fee-charging private schools.

HIGHER EDUCATION

Ireland has seven universities, four of which form the National University of Ireland but maintain independent campuses in Dublin (UCD), Cork (UCC), Galway (NUIG), and Maynooth (NUIM). The oldest and most prestigious university in Ireland is the University of Dublin, better known as Trinity College. Trinity was founded in the sixteenth century and is located in the heart of the city. Ireland's two newest Universities—Dublin City University (DCU) and the University of Limerick (UL)—are less than 20 years old. Competition for places in all of Ireland's universities is very high. Ireland also has a world-renowned medical college, the Royal College of Surgeons (RCSI), which is based in Dublin and which was founded in 1784.

Since the 1970s, Ireland has also developed a number of technology institutes around the country that offer degree-level education in a wide range of technical and applied subject areas. Some of Ireland's more established technical institutes, such as Dublin Institute of Technology (DIT) and Cork Institute of Technology (CIT), are now major competitors to the universities, attracting an increasing number of students. Carlow, Waterford, Dundalk, Sligo, and Athlone are among the other Irish towns with technology institutes.

Education and Health Data

- Life expectancy at birth male: 75
- Life expectancy at birth female: 80
- Infant mortality rate per 1,000: 6
- Under five mortality rate per 1,000: 6
- Physicians per 1,000 people: 2
- Health expenditure as % of GDP: 7%
- Education expenditure as % of GDP: 4%
- Primary school net enrollment: 94%
- Student-teacher ratio, primary: 19
- Adult literacy as % age 15+: 99%

Source: United Nations Agencies and World Bank

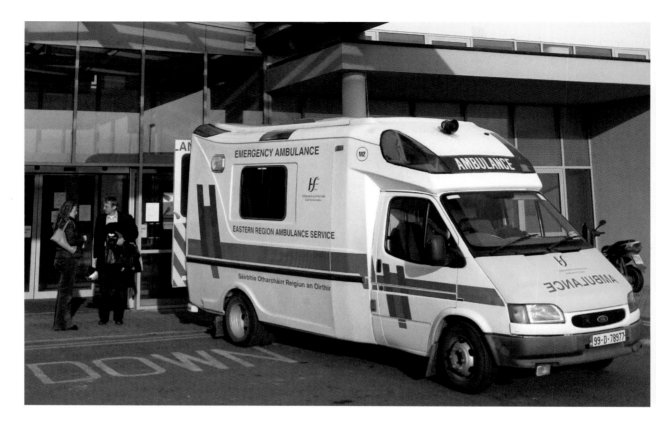

HEALTH CARE

The standard of health care in Ireland is on the same level with that in other parts of western Europe. Ireland's health-care system is the subject of intense public interest as successive governments try to improve its efficiency. The main organizations responsible for health care in Ireland are the Department for Health and Children and the Health Services Executive (HSE), which was created on January 1, 2005. The state provides a basic health care service to all, but almost half the population also pays for private health insurance. Private care gives people better hospital facilities, such as private rooms, and normally means faster access to medical treatment than in the state system. There are few private hospitals in Ireland, however, so nearly all patients (whether public or private) use services provided in public hospitals. Under this system, patients with

▲ An ambulance delivers patients to a hospital in Blanchardstown, located near Dublin.

private insurance tend to be treated sooner. This reduces the services available to uninsured patients and is considered unfair by many. Ireland has about 40 hospitals throughout the country. As part of the restructuring of health care in Ireland, the government began discussing plans for reducing to 12 regional "superhospitals" in 2003. To date, these plans have not been finalized.

PUBLIC AND PRIMARY HEALTH

At a primary care level, most Irish doctors (General Practitioners, or GPs) operate as private businesses and are free to locate wherever they wish. The majority of people pay for a visit to the doctor, with an average cost of U.S.$50 to $63 in 2006. Vulnerable groups, such as the elderly and poor, can receive a General Medical Services (GMS) card under a government program that provides them with free GP and dental treatment. In addition, the HSE provides free essential medical services to the community such as immunization and health screening for illnesses such as cancer or heart disease. Social services such as "meals on wheels," which delivers meals to elderly or homebound people, or home-help services are largely voluntary. These services are provided and funded by religious and charitable organizations.

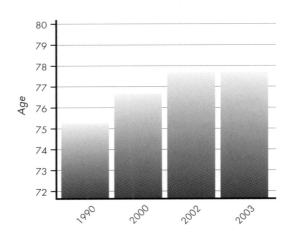

▲ Life expectancy at birth 1990–2003

Focus on: Smoking Ban

One of Ireland's most innovative public health initiatives in recent times is the Public Workplace Smoking Ban. The Smoking Ban (as it came to be known) was introduced in 2004 by Michael Martin, who was then the Minister of Health. The Smoking Ban was intended to improve public health and reduce the inhaling of secondhand smoke by nonsmokers. Smoking was banned in all public buildings, bars, and restaurants. While many expected the Smoking Ban to fail, it has been extremely successful. Most smokers must now leave the building if they wish to smoke or go to special outdoor smoking areas such as those set up by many bars. The success of Ireland's smoking ban has been closely monitored by other countries in Europe. Scotland introduced a similar smoking ban in 2006, and England will follow in 2007. Other countries are also thinking about introducing a public smoking ban.

◀ Following the ban on smoking in public places in Ireland in 2004, many bars created outdoor smoking areas such as this one.

CHAPTER 11

Culture and Religion

Ireland is an overwhelmingly Christian country—about 88 percent of its population is Catholic. The number of regularly practicing Catholics in Ireland, however, has fallen considerably in recent times. A survey in 2006 by the national broadcaster RTÉ found that only 48 percent of people attended Mass (the main Catholic service) at least once a week, compared with 81 percent in 1990.

A high point for many Catholics in Ireland was the visit of Pope John Paul II in 1979, who led a Mass in Dublin's Phoenix Park that was attended by over one million people. Many of Ireland's major festivals are associated with Catholicism and, in particular, with St. Patrick. One of Ireland's main Catholic celebrations is the climb of Croagh Patrick, in County Mayo,

where St. Patrick fasted for 40 days in A.D. 441. The climb takes place on the last Sunday in July and is known locally as Reek Sunday, because this is the nickname for the mountain.

OTHER RELIGIONS

Protestants make up about 2 to 3 percent of the population in Ireland, with the proportion of Protestants higher in the counties that border Northern Ireland and areas such as Laois and Offaly. Other religions have had only small representation in Ireland, but this is changing as new immigrants bring their religions with them. Islam, Eastern Orthodox Christianity, and new forms of African Christianity are all now present, as are various Chinese belief systems. The Jewish population of Ireland has always been small. Once concentrated in an

► Two nuns help each other as they climb Croagh Patrick, located near Westport in County Mayo, during the annual pilgrimage up the mountain.

▲ Irish Jew Raphael Siev runs the Jewish Museum in Dublin and is part of Ireland's dwindling Jewish community. The number of Jews in Ireland has plummeted since the 1950s and is today around 1,100.

area called Little Jerusalem in the Clanbrassil Street and Portobello districts of Dublin, most of Ireland's Jews have relocated to the suburbs, but the area still has a Jewish museum and old kosher bakery.

SECULARISM AND LIBERALISM
With the decline in the number of practicing Catholics in Ireland, combined with several moral and financial scandals within the Catholic Church since the 1980s, Ireland has become a more secular and liberal society. Evidence of this is in the weakening of the once close ties between Catholicism and the governing parties in Ireland. Examples of Ireland's more liberal society include greater use of contraception and higher rates of divorce. Social trends also reflect these changes; the proportion of children in Ireland born out of

wedlock reached 35 percent in 2005. In spite of these changes, the family is still considered the most important social unit in Ireland. Although the country has fewer of them than in the past, large families are not unusual.

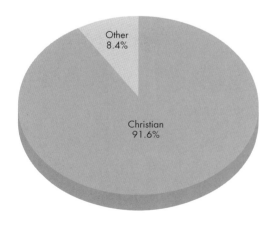

▲ Ireland's major religions

FOOD

Irish cuisine has never been internationally famous and has always tended toward hearty meals based around local ingredients. Potatoes, Irish stew (containing lamb or mutton, potatoes, carrots, and onions), and bacon and cabbage form a major part of the traditional diet. Seafood such as mackerel, salmon, and Dublin

▼ The English Market in Cork is well known for its variety of fresh produce, and it increasingly features organically produced food.

Bay prawns are also important. A range of international foods has become available in Ireland since the 1980s, representing the diversity of cultures now present there. There has also been a renewal of interest in good-quality Irish produce. The country's dairy products and seafood, in particular, are both sold at local farmers' markets in places such as Dublin's Temple Bar and the English Market in Cork and exported around the world.

FESTIVALS AND TRADITIONS

Ireland's biggest national holiday is St. Patrick's Day on March 17. It is celebrated with street parades across the country. Dublin's St. Patrick's Day parade attracts over one million people. Elsewhere, festivals take place all over Ireland throughout the year. Some specialized festivals have gained strong followings in Ireland. These include the Dublin Theater Festival, in October; the Cat Laughs Comedy Festival, in Kilkenny in June; and the Festival of World Cultures, in Dún Laoghaire in August. Ireland's important traditional festivals include the Puc Fair, in Killorglin, in which a wild goat is elected as "King Puc" for the three days of the fair. *Puc* is the Irish word for goat.

THE ARTS

Ireland has a strong heritage in the arts, particularly in literature and drama. Irish writers and dramatists are among the world's best known and include Bram Stoker, James Joyce, Oscar Wilde, Samuel Beckett, George Bernard Shaw, and Sean O'Casey. The Abbey Theater, in Dublin, which opened in 1904, is where many of these writers made their name before going on to worldwide fame. New playwrights such as Martin McDonagh and

Marina Carr, whose plays are widely performed in Ireland and overseas, along with novelists such as Colm Tóibín and John Banville, are among the next wave of Irish writers. Ireland has never had a strong film industry, but small-budget movies made in Ireland have achieved worldwide acclaim. Some of these include *My Left Foot*, *The Commitments,* and *Michael Collins*. Ireland is also popular as a shooting location for movies. The Hollywood blockbusters *Braveheart* and *Saving Private Ryan* were filmed in Ireland.

Focus on: The Irish Language

The Irish language, *Gaelige,* is known in Ireland as "Irish" but is more commonly referred to outside Ireland as Gaelic. It is one of Europe's oldest languages, and it is closely associated with the other Celtic languages, especially Scots Gaelic and Manx. Once spoken nationally, its use suffered when it was outlawed in public life by the Penal Laws of the late seventeenth century and replaced with English. Ireland today has about 100,000 native Irish speakers, most of whom are concentrated in the western counties of Donegal, Mayo, Galway, Kerry, and Cork. This area in which Irish speakers live is known as the *Gaeltacht* and has protected legal status. There are also small *Gaeltacht* areas in Ring, in County Waterford, and Rathcairn, in County Meath. Because Irish is taught in schools in Ireland, most people in the country have a good understanding of the language. Although Irish is not widely used beyond the *Gaeltacht* areas, the language remains strong for cultural and political reasons.

▼ A bilingual (English and *Gaelige*) road sign in Kinsale, in County Cork.

CHAPTER 12

Leisure and Tourism

Leisure and tourism in Ireland are based on the country's beautiful countryside and its cultural traditions. Ireland's landscapes have broad appeal to both visitors and locals. The country's traditional sports remain strong, and Irish folk music and dance have gained worldwide popularity.

GAELIC SPORTS

The Irish have long been a nation of enthusiastic sports followers. The Gaelic Athletic Association (GAA) is one of the biggest organizations in the country. The main GAA sports are Gaelic football and hurling. Gaelic football is played across Ireland. Teams are organized at club and county levels. Women's Gaelic football has become one of Ireland's fastest-growing sports in recent years and is currently played by an estimated 100,000 women and girls. Hurling is one of the fastest field-sports in the world. It is more widely played in southern Ireland. Although unique, hurling mixes elements of field hockey and lacrosse. It is played with a curved ash stick called a *camán* and a hard ball known as a *sliothar*. Women play a game similar to hurling called *camogie*. The other two GAA sports are handball and rounders. Handball is a game similar to squash except that the hand is used to hit the ball rather than a racquet. Rounders is a game similar to baseball.

 Did You Know?

Gaelic football was taken with the Irish when they emigrated abroad. Today, there are Gaelic football teams in London and New York.

◀ Hurling is one of the more popular and widely played Gaelic sports. It is played in Ireland and beyond.

Focus on: Horse Racing

Ireland is well known internationally for horse racing, a sport in which it has achieved great success both in breeding and racing. Racing is now a multimillion-euro industry. The most famous racecourses in Ireland include the Curragh (for flat-racing) and Fairyhouse and Punchestown (for jump-racing). For many Irish racing enthusiasts, the high point of the year is the National Hunt Festival that is held every March in Cheltenham, England. Most of the top jockeys in Britain are Irish. These jockeys also ride internationally, competing in Hong Kong, Dubai, and the famous Breeder's Cup event in the United States. Ireland's horse-breeding industry is strong, and the annual horse sales in County Kildare attract the wealthiest British, Arab, European, and American buyers, who are drawn by the worldwide success of Irish-bred horses.

◀ A horse is paraded during an equestrian show in southeast Ireland.

OTHER SPORTS

Soccer is hugely popular in Ireland, and the country's national team has qualified for World Cup tournaments in 1990, 1994, and 2002. The team's best performance was reaching the quarter-finals in 1990. At the time, the team was run by an English manager, Jack Charlton. Ireland's soccer team has a huge number of followers, with thousands of Irish soccer fans traveling to support their team when it plays overseas. Many of the best Irish soccer players compete in the English leagues. Rugby Union is another popular sport in Ireland, and the country's national team has won the Five Nations championships (with Wales, Scotland, England, and France) several times. In most team sports, Ireland and Northern Ireland have separate teams, but rugby is one of a few sports that has an All-Ireland team, with players from both sides of the border. Other sports with All-Ireland teams include cricket, hockey, and show jumping.

Water-based sports, from windsurfing to sailing in large ocean-going yachts, are also popular. The wild waves on Ireland's western shores also make the country an increasingly popular surfing location, in spite of the relatively cold water. Surfing has a growing following in Ireland, with the best breaks off the beaches of Sligo, Donegal, and Clare.

MUSIC

Ireland is famous for a wide range of musical styles and artists. Many Irish artists are popular today. Authentic traditional Irish music is particularly present in the counties of Galway, Donegal, Kerry, and Clare in the west of Ireland. In County Clare, Doolin and Miltown Malbay are two of Ireland's best-known music centers. In Doolin, visitors go to local pubs to hear Irish tunes played on fiddles, accordions, guitars, and native instruments such as the bodhran, which is a small skin drum, and the uilleann pipes. Some of the biggest names in traditional Irish music are the Chieftains, Planxty, De Dannan, Altan, Sharon Shannon, and Danú. Traditional Irish music and dance are popular around the world, as shown by hit shows such as *Riverdance*.

Contemporary Irish music includes leading pop and rock acts, some of whom have achieved global appeal. The rock band U2 are by far the best-known Irish act and one of the biggest bands in the world. Formed in the late 1970s by four young Dubliners, U2 performed in Dublin in 2005 for the first time in 16 years to a total audience of 250,000 people over three days. Van Morrison, the Cranberries, the Corrs, Sinéad O'Connor, Clannad, Thin Lizzy, and Boyzone are among other international acts that have

▼ People relax and enjoy playing and listening to traditional Irish music in a bar in Duncannon.

emerged from Ireland. This musical legacy feeds a host of musical talent in the country. Ireland's domestic music scene is thriving, and going to live concerts is a popular leisure activity.

TOURISM IN IRELAND

Tourism has been a significant part of the Irish economy since the 1960s. Visitors from the United States, Britain, and elsewhere in Europe make up the majority of Ireland's tourists. This is partially a result of historical links, with many British and American tourists coming to Ireland to visit family members or ancestral homes. Ireland's wild and attractive landscapes as well as its reputation for friendly and welcoming people help make it popular with a wide range of visitors, especially with the increase of low-cost flights from mainland Europe. Since 2000, however, the growth in the number of visitors to the country has slowed. Reasons for this include the cost of accommodations, lack of good food, poor transportation, and an unpredictable climate. Dublin continues to receive high visitor numbers and has long been the country's most frequently visited area. One goal of the Irish Tourist Board is to persuade tourists to explore the rest of the country in order to spread both the pressures and benefits of tourism more

▲ A tourist reads about the attractions in the town of Wexford. Improved visitor information, such as this board, is helping to spread tourism beyond Dublin.

Tourism in Ireland

- 📂 Tourist arrivals, millions: 6.774
- 📂 Earnings from tourism in U.S.$: 5,265,000,000
- 📂 Tourism as % foreign earnings: 4.1%
- 📂 Tourist departures, millions: 4.634
- 📂 Expenditure on tourism in U.S.$: 4,832,000,000

Source: World Bank

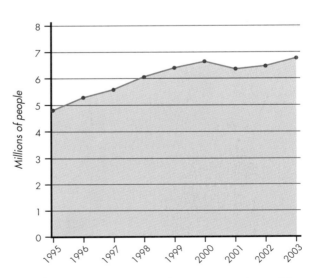

▲ Changes in international tourism, 1995–2003

CHAPTER 13

Environment and Conservation

In spite of its modest size, Ireland has a wide range of habitats, including forests, bogs, mountains, cliffs, rivers, and coasts. Ireland is an important stop-off point for many species of migratory birds, but the country's wildlife is limited, with only a few native species. Pressure on Ireland's environment comes almost entirely from human activities. Ireland has few places not affected by humans, but the country is encouraging the protection of its environment through a range of practical actions.

AN ISLAND TRANSFORMED

Historically, forests and peat bogs covered much of Ireland's landscape. Beginning in the Middle Ages, pressure for timber, fuel, and agricultural land meant that vast areas of forest were felled, peat land harvested, and bogs drained. Today, original forest covers less than 1 percent of Ireland's land area; agricultural land (sometimes mixed with forest or other natural habitats) accounts for up to 91 percent. With natural habitats squeezed into a few remaining pockets, their importance to the country's wildlife and their need for protection are increasing. Ireland's protected areas are designated as either Natural Heritage Areas (NHA), Special Areas of Conservation (SAC), or Special Protection Areas (SPA). Much of Ireland's six national parks—Killarney, Glenveagh, Connemara, Wicklow Mountains, the Burren, and Ballycroy—includes land designated as an SAC.

One of the problems in protecting land in Ireland is that most of it is privately owned, and the government cannot afford to purchase land to set aside for national parks or other forms of protection. To overcome this problem, Ireland's government departments work closely with

◀ This stunning scenery surrounds Upper Lake, in Killarney National Park. Upper Lake is one of the three lakes of Killarney; the other two are Muckross Lake (Middle Lake) and Lough Leane (Lower Lake).

► Connemara ponies in the countryside at the Bog of Letterdife, near Roundstone in County Galway.

landowners through incentives and management plans. For example, Ireland's government works with landowners to plant about 50,000 acres (20,000 hectares) of trees annually between 2000 and 2030, with the hope of increasing forest cover in the country by about 1 percent every three years.

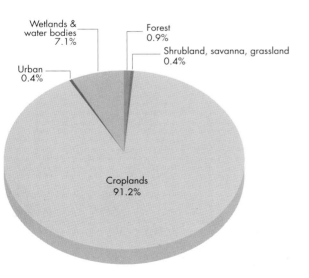

▲ Types of habitat

WILDLIFE

Ireland's native birdlife is not diverse compared to birdlife in other European nations, but its coastal waters and wetlands serve as habitats for bird species making their annual migrations between northern and southern latitudes. Ireland has some of the largest colonies of breeding seabirds anywhere in the world. These include fulmars, petrels, puffins, and razorbills, as well as a variety of gulls. The majority of these birds nest on the cliffs of western Ireland. On the east coast of Ireland, wading birds are more common, particularly around Dublin Bay.

Ireland's 25 mammal species include three species of deer (red, fallow, and sika), hares, rabbits, and the red fox. The Connemara pony is a native Irish horse that has been domesticated into a riding pony. Twenty-three species of whale or dolphin have been identified in Ireland's waters. On the country's western coast, people on land can often get a good look at whales and dolphins in the water.

◀ Nitrogenous algae clog the waters of Lough Leane in County Kerry. The algae has been caused by run-off from nitrate fertilizers used on farmland around the lake.

AIR AND WATER QUALITY

Besides habitat loss, the main threats to Ireland's wildlife come from poor air and water quality. Agriculture, industry, and especially transportation are the country's main sources of pollutants, and the rapid economic growth of Ireland since the 1980s has increased levels of pollution. Controls on high-polluting fuels, such as coal, were introduced in the 1990s in response to increased pollution. As a result, emissions from factories, homes, and power stations have declined considerably. Emissions from transportation, however, continue to rise and cause great problems where traffic jams occur. Emissions from traffic jams can be up to 250 percent higher than when traffic is flowing. Ireland's water quality has also improved in recent years, with the last national survey (1998–2000) showing that 70 percent of its rivers and 85 percent of its lakes were in

Environmental and Conservation Data

📁 Forested area as % total land area: 0.9%

📁 Protected area as % total land area: 1.3%

📁 Number of protected areas: 104

SPECIES DIVERSITY

Category	Known species	Threatened species
Mammals	25	5
Breeding birds	143	1
Reptiles	6	n/a
Amphibians	4	n/a
Fish	365	n/a
Plants	950	1

Source: World Resources Institute

satisfactory condition. The continued threat to the quality of Ireland's water comes primarily from agricultural run-off that includes pesticides, fertilizers, and animal wastes.

WASTE AND RECYCLING

Waste is one of the biggest environmental challenges facing Ireland, because it has limited options for disposal. The country's landfills are rapidly filling up—just 8 years of capacity were left in 2005—and incineration is unpopular with communities concerned about toxic emissions. Recycling is important in Ireland; in 2005, the country's government passed a plan to recycle 35 percent of municipal waste by 2013. Ireland has an extensive network of recycling facilities that includes more than 1,900 drop-off centers (for example, in supermarkets), 69 civic waste-and-recycling facilities, and numerous curbside collection programs. In 2004, almost one-half of all commercial waste (much of it packaging material) was also recovered for recycling or reuse. The country's government is developing new plans to reduce the amount of waste the country produces, for example, by reconsidering the use of packaging. Ireland is also working to improve the recycling of its organic waste, which remains poor by European standards.

Focus on: Plastic Bags

On March 4, 2002, a new tax on plastic shopping bags passed into law in Ireland. All retailers were required to charge shoppers about U.S.$0.20 for each plastic shopping bag they used. The tax was introduced as an incentive to reduce the number of plastic bags entering the waste stream in Ireland. The money raised by the tax was used to pay for a special environment fund. The impact of the tax on plastic bags was almost immediate; the use of plastic bags fell by more than 90 percent within three months. Shoppers quickly became used to carrying strong reusable shopping bags that many retailers sold for about U.S.$1.25 each. Ireland's tax on plastic bags is expected to reduce the number of plastic bags used in the country by more than one billion bags every year.

▶ Most people in Ireland now use strong reusable plastic bags to carry their shopping.

CHAPTER 14

Future Challenges

Ireland has undergone a period of rapid change since the mid-1980s during which its economy has transformed, its society and culture become more liberal and diverse, and its quality of life improved considerably. It has also seen growing inequalities, increased traffic congestion, rapid population growth, and increased environmental pressures. The challenge ahead is for Ireland to balance the rewards of success more evenly and build a sustainable platform for the future.

SPREADING THE LOAD

Dublin has been the engine of economic growth in Ireland for the past 50 years. The city's population is naturally clustered in the Greater Dublin area, creating enormous pressure for services and degrading both the environment and people's quality of life. In November 2002, Ireland's government launched a 20-year plan, the National Spatial Strategy (NSS), aimed at resolving this imbalance. The NSS is designed to integrate the country's need for greater environmental protection with its continuing need for economic and social development. The key to this strategy is greater regional development to make the areas beyond Dublin more attractive for economic activity and living. This will be done through regional incentives to help create employment opportunities and the strengthening of services at a regional level. If successful, the

◀ This aerial picture of Dublin shows the River Liffey. A key challenge for Ireland is to spread its future growth and prosperity beyond the capital city.

NSS will reduce levels of commuting and, therefore, traffic congestion, and make the most of Ireland's regional centers to boosting growing industries, such as tourism.

ADAPTABILITY

Ireland's ability to adapt to changing influences from outside the country will be vital to its future. With the expansion of the EU in 2004, for example, Ireland moved from an era in which it was one of the main recipients of EU aid into an era in which it is no longer the most needy member of the EU family. At the same time, the newfound freedoms of the EU are opening Ireland to a new wave of economic migrants coming to Ireland in the hope of finding work in its booming economy. This will place pressure on the country's services and housing. It may also lead to increased competition for jobs between immigrants and local people, especially because new immigrants may be willing to work for considerably lower wages.

INEQUALITIES

Ensuring that as many people as possible share in the wealth and future of Ireland presents the country's government with great challenges. For example, the country's health-care system is still considered to favor those with higher incomes who are able to afford health insurance. Housing is another area in which inequalities are highly visible, with housing becoming too expensive for many lower-income families. Policies such

as the NSS and the National Development Plan are designed to reduce inequalities by spreading out the country's population—and also the pressures on Ireland's housing and services—to areas beyond Dublin, but their impact has yet to be fully realized.

▼ Immigrants from Asia shop in Dublin's busy Moore Street Market. Refugees and economic migrants continue to add to the diversity of Ireland's population.

Time Line

c. 6000–5000 B.C. Ancient tribes live in Ireland.

c. 3200 B.C. Newgrange burial monument built.

c. A.D. 432 St. Patrick comes to Ireland and introduces Christianity.

c. 800–1000 Period of Viking invasions and settlement.

1014 Brian Boru, the Irish High King, defeats the Vikings at Battle of Clontarf.

1169 Anglo-Norman soldiers under King Henry II of England arrive and begin a British presence in Ireland.

c. 1200 English control much of Ireland from their base in Dublin.

1550s Plantations (settlements) in west and south, especially in Queen's and King's counties (Laois and Offaly).

1610s Great Plantation of Ulster.

1649 Drogheda massacre by Oliver Cromwell's forces.

1691 Penal Laws are introduced by the English to suppress and control the Irish (and, specifically Irish Catholics).

1745 Newry Canal built–first canal in British Isles.

1785 The British allow the formation of the first Irish parliament (Grattan's Parliament).

1798 Uprising against continued British control of Ireland.

1801 Act of Union makes Ireland part of the United Kingdom.

1821 A 2,000-year-old human body is found at Gallagh Bog in County Galway.

1829 Catholic emancipation and the end of the Penal Laws.

1838 First railway opens in Ireland.

1845–1847 The Great Famine. Potato blight leads to crop failure and the deaths of over one million people.

1867 Uprising against British control by the Fenians, a group that wants Irish independence.

1884 The Gaelic Athletic Association (GAA) is founded.

1912 Early plans to allow home rule for Ireland are discussed.

1916 (April) Week-long rebellion against British rule by Irish Republican Brotherhood in which the General Post Office and other prominent Dublin buildings are seized.

1919 Irish political party Sinn Féin declares first independent *Dáil* (parliament) of Ireland.

1919–1921 War of Independence between Britain and Ireland.

1921 Ceasefire in the War of Independence leads to the political division of Ireland into Northern Ireland (which remained part of the UK) and the Irish Free State.

1922–1923 Irish Civil War.

1937 Irish Free State renamed Eire.

1949 Eire renamed Republic of Ireland.

1965 Ireland signs Anglo-Irish Free Trade Agreement with Britain to boost its economy.

1968–1969 Civil rights marches by Catholic minorities in Northern Ireland lead to violence with Protestant communities.

1969 British army moves into Northern Ireland to try to restore peace between Catholics and Protestants.

1973 Ireland becomes a member of the European Economic Community (the European Union after 1992).

1979 Visit by Pope John Paul II to Ireland.

1985 Low-cost air passenger carrier Ryanair is founded.

1987 Creation of the IFSC (Irish Financial Services Center) in Dublin with support from the EEC.

1990 Ireland's soccer team reaches the quarter-finals of the World Cup. Mary Robinson becomes the first female president of Ireland.

1993 Downing Street Declaration assures Protestants in Northern Ireland of right to vote on any unification with the Republic of Ireland.

1994 Ceasefire announced by the IRA (Irish Republican Army).

1997 Irish President Mary Robinson leaves office to become UN High Commissioner for Human Rights (until 2002).

1998 (April 10) Good Friday Agreement sets Northern Ireland on the path to self-government.

2002 Euro currency replaces the Irish punt as the official currency of Ireland. Disputes lead to collapse of Northern Ireland Assembly; UK government retakes control.

2004 European Union (EU) expands from 15 to 25 members. Luas light-rail system opens in Dublin.

2005 IRA completes decommissioning of weapons. Cork celebrates being the European Capital of Culture.

2007 European Union (EU) expands from 25 to 27 members.

Glossary

asylum seeker someone who seeks shelter from persecution or danger in a country other than his or her own

blight a disease of plants (often caused by a fungus) that causes them to wither and die; in Ireland, blight led to the failure of the potato crop in 1845–1847

Catholic a person who belongs to the Roman Catholic Church, which is based in Vatican City and has the pope as the head of the church

Celtic relating to a group of languages (and associated cultures) that include Breton, Welsh, Cornish, Scottish, Irish, Gaelic, and Manx

chieftain the leader of a group of people; used to describe the leaders of Ireland's historical tribal groups

civil rights a set of rights that all members of a society should enjoy equally, such as the right to vote, freedom of speech and mobility, and fair treatment from the law

coalition a union of two or more political parties which join forces to create a majority that is able to form a government

convict someone who has been convicted, or found guilty, of a crime

decommission to take something out of working order; in Ireland, often used to refer to the IRA decommissioning (destroying) its weapons

depopulation the process by which an area such as a city, region, or country loses its population

discriminate to treat people differently and, often, unequally

emigrate to leave your country of origin to live or work in another country

euro a common currency shared by 12 countries in Europe; the euro was adopted in January 2002

fossil fuel one of any energy-rich substances formed from the decayed remains of plants and animals that died millions of years ago, including oil, coal, gas, and peat

Gaelic relating to the Gaels (Celts from Scotland, Ireland or the Isle of Man who speak the Gaelic language); used to describe elements of their shared culture, such as language and sports

hydroelectric power (HEP) electricity generated by the power of water passing through a turbine

ice age a period of colder climatic conditions when much of the northern hemisphere was covered in ice

incineration to dispose of by burning; used as a method of waste disposal

infrastructure the transportation, communications, energy, and other networks and systems that help an economy function efficiently

Mass the service of Communion (commemoration of Jesus Christ's last supper); Mass is one of the most important services of the Roman Catholic Church

migratory regularly traveling over large distances as part of an annual survival pattern; used to refer to birds or animals that have such patterns

missionary someone sent to another country by a church to spread its beliefs or to carry out social work such as teaching or medicine

nationalization the process of bringing something (such as land or an industry) under the control of the state rather than private owners

nominate to suggest someone for a position of power or control

nondenominational not relating to any religious group

nongovernmental organization (NGO) an organization that operates independently of the government of the country in which it is based

paramilitary having to do with an organization that is modeled on military principles but not officially part of a military

partition the process of dividing a country into parts

peat a fossil fuel composed of decayed plant matter that is high in energy and is burned to generate electricity or heat

penal colony a place where criminals were sent to complete their punishment; Australia was originally used as a penal colony by Britain

plantation a large estate or settlement controlled by one or a few people

Presbyterian having to do with or belonging to the Presbyterian Church

proportional representation (PR) a system of democratic voting in which candidates are elected to office according to the proportion of the vote they receive

Protestant a member of one of the Christian churches that rejects the authority of the pope as the leader of the Christian faith

Republican in Ireland, a person who believes that Northern Ireland should be politically unified with the Republic of Ireland and cease to be part of the UK

ria a physical landscape feature where a former river valley is submerged by the ocean; rias are common along the west coast of Ireland and account for this region's craggy, indented shape

run-off liquid waste or waste that is transported in water; run-off is normally generated by agriculture or industry such as through use of farming chemicals that run into nearby rivers and streams

service industry an industry that provides a service to people and other industries; banking, insurance, transportation, education, and health care are examples of service industries

sustainable having to do with practices intended to make sure that resources will still be intact for future generations

Taoiseach an old Irish title meaning chieftain or leader that is Ireland's head of government and is the equivalent of the prime minister in other countries

turbine a mechanical device that is used to convert the movement of water, steam, or wind into electrical energy

urbanization the process by which a place becomes increasingly dominated by urban, or built-up, spaces as opposed to natural landscapes

vocational having to do with education that teaches skills that relate to a particular job or career

Further Information

BOOKS TO READ

Cottrell, Robert C. *Northern Ireland and England: The Troubles* (Arbitrary Borders: Political Boundaries in World History). Chelsea House, 2004.

Friedman, Lita. *Mary Robinson: Fighter for Human Rights* (Avisson Young Adult Series). Avisson Press, 2004.

Gallagher, Carol S. *The Irish Potato Famine* (Great Disasters: Reforms and Ramifications). Chelsea House, 2001.

Hogan, Edward Patrick and Erin Hogan Fouberg. *Ireland* (Modern World Nations). Chelsea House, 2003.

Hossell, Karen Price. *Irish Americans* (Immigrants in America). Lucent Books, 2003.

Levy, Patricia Marjorie. *Ireland* (Cultures of the World). Benchmark Books, 2004.

Llywelyn, Morgan. *Brian Boru: Emperor of the Irish* (Celtic World of Morgan Llywelyn). Tor Books, 1997.

Spencer, Shannon. *Ireland* (Countries of the World). Gareth Stevens, 2000.

Woolf, Alex. *Focus on the United Kingdom* (World in Focus). World Almanac Library, 2006.

USEFUL WEB SITES

BBC News Country Profile: Ireland
news.bbc.co.uk/1/hi/world/europe/country_profiles/1038581.stm

CIA World Factbook: Ireland
www.cia.gov/publications/factbook/geos/ei.html#Trans

Football Association of Ireland
www.fai.ie

Ireland: Information on the Irish State
www.irlgov.ie

Irish Rugby Football Union
www.irishrugby.ie

World Almanac for Kids: Ireland
www.worldalmanacforkids.com/explore/nations/ireland.html

Publisher's note to educators and parents: Our editors have carefully reviewed these Web sites to ensure that they are suitable for children. Many Web sites change frequently, however, and we cannot guarantee that a site's future contents will continue to meet our high standards of quality and educational value. Be advised that children should be closely supervised whenever they access the Internet.

Index

About the Authors

Rob Bowden is a freelance educational writer and photographer with a background in teaching geography and development studies. He has written and advised on many educational books and specializes in global environmental and social issues.

Dr. Ronan Foley has been a Lecturer in the Department of Geography of NUI Maynooth, in Ireland, since 2003. His areas of specialization are historical geography, health geography, and GIS. He has also written books on world health and the River Rhine.